PLANET EARTH

SHEILA PADGET

MACDONALD

Editor Jan Burgess
Designer Peter Luff

Illustrated by:
Drawing Attention/Robert Burns
Phillip Ems
Richard Hook
David Kerr
Mike Roffe
Ray Turvey
Chris Warner

Published for Kmart Corporation
Troy, Michigan 48084

© Theorem Publishing Limited 1980
Conceived and produced by
Theorem Publishing Limited
71-73 Great Portland Street
London W1N 5DH

First published in 1980 by
Macdonald Educational Ltd
Holywell House
Worship Street
London EC2A 2EN

ISBN 0 356 07091 3

Printed in Hong Kong

Key to cover

1. It is easier to venture into space than to penetrate the crust of our own planet. Find out what lies beneath our feet on pages 8 and 9.

2. Scientists use satellites to help them forecast the weather more accurately. You too can be a weather forecaster. To find out how, see pages 30 and 31.

3. A million years ago huge ice sheets covered large areas of our planet. How do we know this? Has the ice now retreated for ever, or are we due for another ice age? Read pages 20 and 21 to find out.

4. Rocks are the earth's building block How are they formed? What causes s weird shapes to develop in the gloom of underground caverns? Read abou rocks on pages 12 and 13.

5. Volcanoes are the most spectacula of all earth's natural phenomena. The build mountains, form islands and create new crust. Read more about volcanoes on pages 10 and 11.

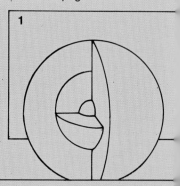

PLANET EARTH

To find out about our planet, you simply have to look around you – at the landscape, the kinds of rocks and pebbles on the ground, the rivers and lakes in your neighbourhood. This book can help you make sense of what you see. It tells you how the rocks were formed in the first place, what effect the weather has on the earth, why rivers behave the way they do. You can also read about aspects of the earth that you probably won't be able to see on your doorstep – the volcano that grew in a farmer's cornfield, why earthquakes happen, what it's like to live on the ice caps. Turn to the back of the book for more ideas on how to find out about the earth.

CONTENTS

The Earth in Space	4
A Planet with a Difference	6
The Violent Earth	8
Rings of Fire	10
Earth's Building Blocks	12
Ups and Downs	14
Wet and Windy!	16
Rivers, Lakes and Marshes	18
Icebound!	20
The Empty Lands	22
The Teeming Forests	24
Inner Space	26
The Energy Storehouse	28
Finding out about the Earth	30
Index	32

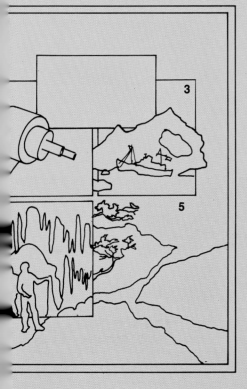

The Earth in Space

For centuries people believed the earth was the centre of the universe. We now know that our planet is only a minute part of this immense void. If you have ever tried to count the stars at night you will have realized that space is impossible to measure. The earth is one of nine planets that orbit the sun. Together the sun and planets make up our solar system, which is just a small part of the galaxy of the Milky Way. The sun itself is only one of *100,000 million* stars in the Milky Way – and there are millions of other galaxies in the universe!

Nobody knows exactly how the earth was formed. Some scientists believe that a huge cloud of space dust and gases began to spiral. The outer dense materials condensed and combined to form the planets. The inner lighter materials contracted to form the sun.

Elephants and earthquakes

Primitive people knew nothing of science and therefore invented explanations for anything they could not understand. One Hindu legend said that the earth stood on a golden plate supported on the backs of elephants whose movements caused earthquakes. The elephants stood on a turtle representing the water-god Vishnu.

Down the plughole

Watch your bath water drain away. In the northern hemisphere the water runs away in an anti–clockwise direction. The earth's rotation causes the water at the southern end of the bath to move through space faster than the water at the northern end. So the water itself begins to rotate. It moves in the opposite direction in the southern hemisphere, and on the equator the water runs straight down the plughole without spiralling.

Earth rise as seen from the moon as the moon lander takes off to rejoin the Apollo command module. Space travel has given us the final proof that the earth is round.

The earth makes two movements in space. It spins on its own axis (a line joining the poles through the centre of the earth) and at the same time it travels round the sun. Each complete spin of the earth on its axis takes 24 hours. At any time only half the earth is turned towards the sun and receiving its light. This gives us day and night.

The earth spins from west to east but because of its shape it spins at different speeds. As the earth is fattest at the equator it moves faster here than to the north or south. At the equator the earth is travelling eastwards at about 1000 miles per hour. Towards the poles where the earth is not so fat it moves more slowly, as it has less distance to go in each complete turn. (This explains the strange behaviour of bath water – in countries north of the equator, the bath water flies through space faster at the southern end than at the northern end. So when the plug is pulled out the water tends to revolve in an anti-clockwise direction. Of course, it works the other way round south of the equator.) The earth takes 365¼ days to complete each orbit round the sun. This is the length of an earth year.

Land of the midnight sun

The movement of the earth around the sun combined with the tilt of the earth's axis gives us the different seasons. The earth is not always tilted in the same direction towards the sun. In the northern hemisphere the sun is directly overhead at the Tropic of Cancer on 21st June, which is midsummer day. There are more hours of daylight than darkness during the summer. The length of daylight increases towards the north until around the North Pole there are 24 hours of daylight. This enables the Eskimo to fish by the light of the midnight sun. By 22nd December midwinter in the northern hemisphere, the sun is directly overhead at the Tropic of Capricorn in the southern hemisphere. Only when the sun is directly overhead at the equator is the length of day and night equal everywhere on earth. This happens twice a year at the spring and autumn equinoxes.

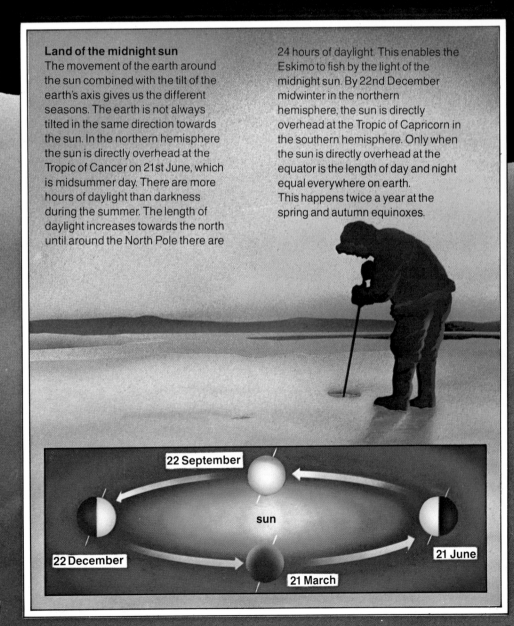

22 September

22 December

sun

21 March

21 June

A Planet with a Difference

Among the planets of the solar system, the earth is alone in supporting life. An infinite variety of living organisms has gradually evolved from the first simple bacteria. The main reason for this is the earth's unique position in the solar system. Lying some 90 million miles from the sun, the earth is at just the right distance to receive life-giving energy from the sun without being scorched by its intense heat. It is also fortunate in having an atmosphere; the earth's gravity prevents this from escaping out into space. The atmosphere contains a high proportion (21%) of oxygen, built up over millions of years. This is the air we breathe. A dense layer of oxygen, called the ozone, has accumulated in the atmosphere. This is vital to life as it filters out the sun's harmful ultraviolet rays.

Out of a violent world...
The first stirrings of life on earth probably began about 3,500 million years ago. The planet then was very different. Surrounding clouds of water vapour had condensed to form hot seething seas. Volcanoes erupted violently. The primitive atmosphere consisted of swirling clouds of hydrogen, carbon monoxide, ammonia and methane and there was little or no oxygen. This mixture allowed intense ultraviolet rays from the sun to bathe the earth's surface. Electrical storms bombarded the planet with lightning.

The thin lifeline
All life on earth is confined to the biosphere, a narrow band around the earth, extending from the lowest layers of the atmosphere to the upper waters of the oceans. On land it goes down only as far as burrowing animals and the roots of plants can reach. Mount Everest is 29,028 feet high, yet at its summit the air is too thin for people to live. At the deepest part of the ocean the pressure is so great human beings can only exist protected by an armoured diving bell. All life depends on energy received from the sun in the form of heat. Plants use this to make their own food in a process called photosynthesis.

How old is old?
The earth is probably about 4,500 million years old. The oldest rocks geologists have identified up to now are about 3,900 million years. Radioactive dating is used to date such rocks. Some radioactive minerals disintegrate at a known rate, so by measuring the amount of these minerals a rock contains, its approximate age can be calculated. We can more accurately date rocks from about 700 million years ago by examining their fossils.

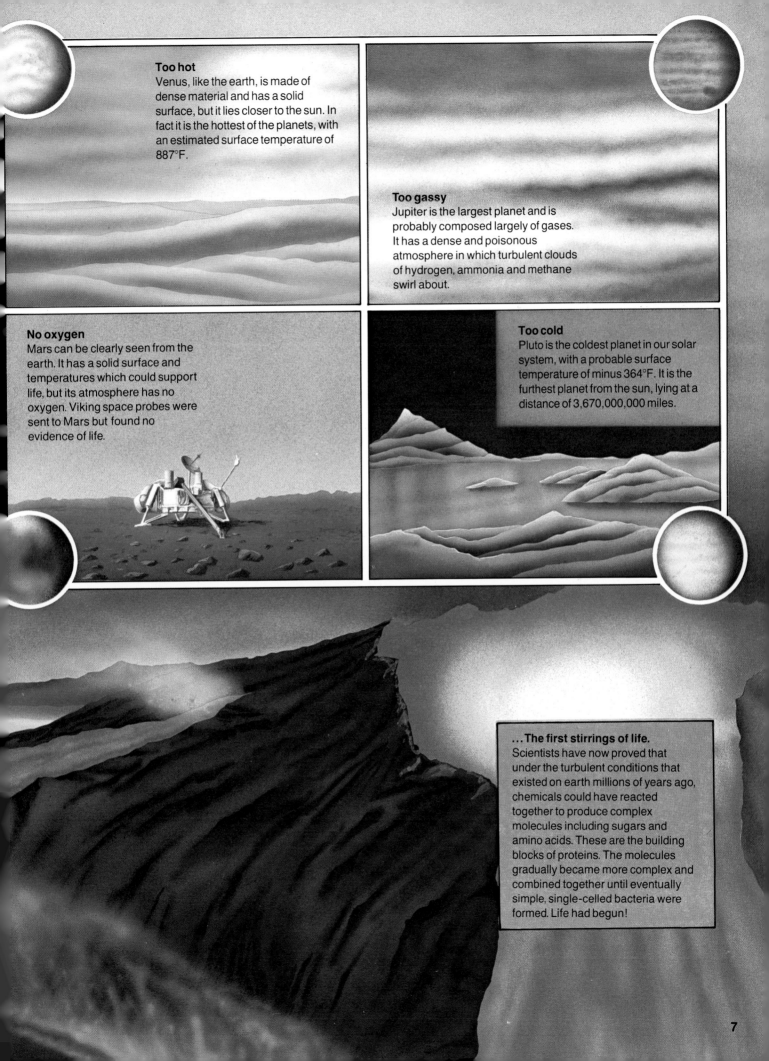

Too hot
Venus, like the earth, is made of dense material and has a solid surface, but it lies closer to the sun. In fact it is the hottest of the planets, with an estimated surface temperature of 887°F.

Too gassy
Jupiter is the largest planet and is probably composed largely of gases. It has a dense and poisonous atmosphere in which turbulent clouds of hydrogen, ammonia and methane swirl about.

No oxygen
Mars can be clearly seen from the earth. It has a solid surface and temperatures which could support life, but its atmosphere has no oxygen. Viking space probes were sent to Mars but found no evidence of life.

Too cold
Pluto is the coldest planet in our solar system, with a probable surface temperature of minus 364°F. It is the furthest planet from the sun, lying at a distance of 3,670,000,000 miles.

...The first stirrings of life.
Scientists have now proved that under the turbulent conditions that existed on earth millions of years ago, chemicals could have reacted together to produce complex molecules including sugars and amino acids. These are the building blocks of proteins. The molecules gradually became more complex and combined together until eventually simple, single-celled bacteria were formed. Life had begun!

Drilling through the earth's crust

In 1962 American scientists began the Mohole project. The idea was to drill 6 miles through the crust to examine the rocks of the mantle. Drilling was done off the Californian coast as the crust is thinner beneath the oceans. The project was later abandoned. The junction between the crust and the mantle is called the Moho after the Yugoslav Mohorovičić who discovered it in 1909.

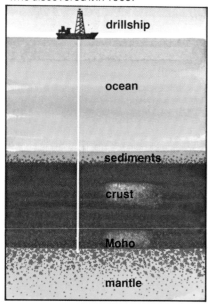

drillship

ocean

sediments

crust

Moho

mantle

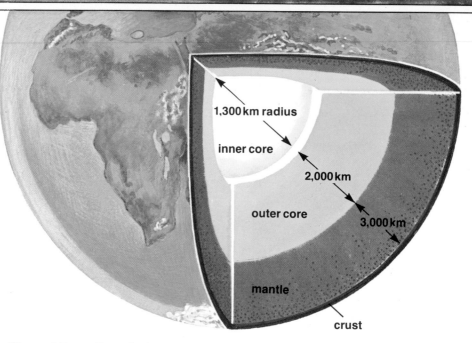

1,300 km radius

inner core

2,000 km

outer core

3,000 km

mantle

crust

The world beneath our feet

We know very little about the interior of our planet. Its outer rocky layer is called the crust. The rocks of the crust are composed mainly of silicon, magnesium and aluminium.

The crust is extremely thin, some 40 miles below the mountains but as little as 3 miles under the oceans. In relation to its size the skin of an apple is thicker than the earth's crust. Below this lie the heavier rocks of the mantle. The earth's core is probably made of nickel and iron. The outer core is thought to be molten (liquid) due to intense heat. However the inner core is probably solid because of the great pressure it is under.

Taming an earthquake?

San Francisco lies on the San Andreas fault. This is where the Pacific and American plates slide past one another. In 1906 a disastrous earthquake destroyed the old city. Smaller earthquakes have happened since. Experiments are being made to see if by 'locking' the plates together, water can be pumped into the fault to 'oil' its movement so that only a minor 'safe' earthquake is caused.

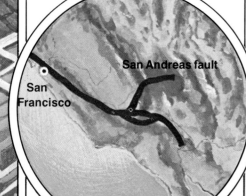

San Andreas fault

San Francisco

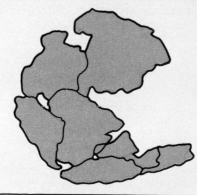

1

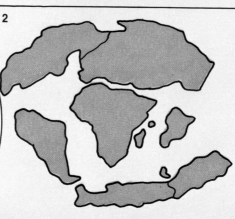

2

Jigsaw puzzle

About 200 million years ago the earth had just one enormous supercontinent – Pangaea (1). Then movement of the crustal plates broke this up (2) and began to pull the continents apart into their present positions. How do we know this? For one thing, the type of rocks found in Africa and South America would match very neatly if the continents were pushed back together again.

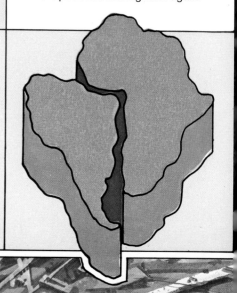

8

The Violent Earth

Earthquakes are a series of rapid shock waves in the earth's crust. Severe earthquakes are usually accompanied by loud rumblings. They may be triggered off by extreme weather such as torrential rain or strong winds. During an earthquake great gaps or fissures open in the ground. These may remain as huge scars across the landscape. Often the ground is moved vertically. In the Alaskan earthquake in 1899, a section of cliff was raised up 45 feet!

Most of the world's earthquakes occur in the same well defined belts as volcanoes (see page 11). Scientists think the earth's crust is broken into a number of plates similar to the pieces of a jigsaw puzzle. These plates are constantly moving and jostling each other. Where two plates slide past one another, tension and friction builds up until an earthquake occurs and releases the pent-up energy.

All fall down?
Traditionally, Japanese houses have been built of light materials which do little harm to the inhabitants if they cave in during a violent earthquake. Large modern buildings have extremely secure foundations. They are made of reinforced materials that sway but do not collapse in an earthquake.

Earthquakes large and small
On average there are about four earthquakes a day. Most of these are so slight they can only be detected by sensitive instruments called seismographs. Many earthquakes occur at sea where they do little damage. However every year there are perhaps three or four earthquakes that cause considerable damage. In populated areas their effects can be devastating. In the Peruvian earthquake in 1970, 50,000 people were killed and a million left homeless. Much of the damage is caused by fires which rage unchecked. The earthquake fractures gas and water mains and brings down electricity cables.

Who spilt the sugar?
The shock waves caused by earthquakes can have strange effects. Minor vertical shocks can empty the sugar from a bowl without moving the bowl! Horizontal shock waves can cause statues to rotate on their pedestals. At the height of an earthquake, shock waves coming from different directions cause the ground to heave and ripple so it looks like a storm-tossed sea. When the earthquake dies down torn roads and buckled railway lines are left.

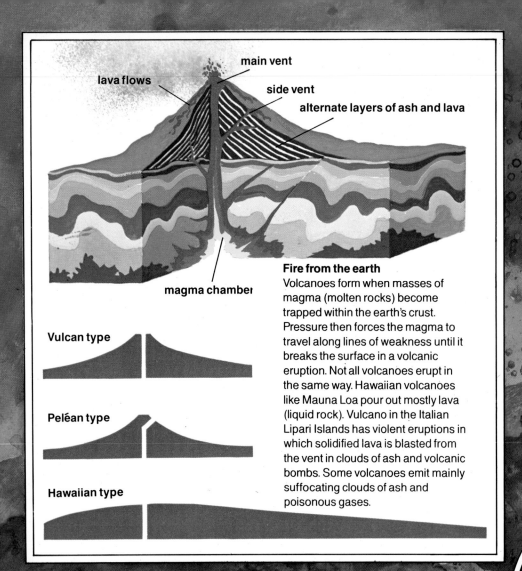

main vent

lava flows

side vent

alternate layers of ash and lava

magma chamber

Vulcan type

Peléan type

Hawaiian type

Fire from the earth

Volcanoes form when masses of magma (molten rocks) become trapped within the earth's crust. Pressure then forces the magma to travel along lines of weakness until it breaks the surface in a volcanic eruption. Not all volcanoes erupt in the same way. Hawaiian volcanoes like Mauna Loa pour out mostly lava (liquid rock). Vulcano in the Italian Lipari Islands has violent eruptions in which solidified lava is blasted from the vent in clouds of ash and volcanic bombs. Some volcanoes emit mainly suffocating clouds of ash and poisonous gases.

Spring 1965

An island is born

Early autumn 1963 Fishermen sailing south of Iceland were puzzled to notice that the sea was hot and glowing.

November 1963 A volcano broke the surface to create a new island. It was named Surtsey after Surtur, a giant who fought with fire.

January 1964

November 1963

February 1964

First few months of life Many scientists came to watch Surtsey's spectacular performance. Clouds of dust and steam hurtled upwards while lava bombs rained down into the sea. Overhead lightning flashed and thunder roared. At night Surtsey looked like a great pillar of fire.

By early 1964 A cone had formed over 300 feet high.

February 1964 A second vent opened from which more lava streamed.

February 1965 The island had grown to over a square mile in size.

Spring 1965 Surtsey became quieter. Soon birds, winds and ocean currents brought seed and life to the island.

Rings of Fire

Volcanoes are the most spectacular of all the earth's natural phenomena. Before an eruption there are usually rumbles, earth tremors and thunder, heralding the approaching danger. Most of the casualties caused by volcanoes are the result of suffocation. When Mount Pelée in Martinique erupted in 1902 a great cloud of hot, poisonous gases shot down the mountainside with hurricane force. In a few seconds 30,000 people were dead.

An eruption releases the pressure that has built up among the molten rock and gases inside the earth's crust. Then the volcano becomes quiet for a while. The plug in the mouth of the volcano may cool and solidify, sealing in the gases and magma. Most volcanoes, like Vesuvius, go through a succession of eruptions at regular intervals before eventually becoming extinct.

volcano
plate edges

Volcanic seas

Volcanoes, like earthquakes, are associated with the movement of the crustal plates. There are so many volcanoes around the Pacific that this area is called the 'Great Ring of Fire'. Many eruptions also occur under the sea. As the plates pull apart new rock wells up to fill the gap.

Birth of a volcano

Parícutin was born on 20 February 1943. While ploughing his cornfield a Mexican farmer felt the ground shake and noticed smoke escaping from a furrow. Just before 4 p.m. an earthquake tore the ground. Explosions and a great cloud of steam, dust and ash followed. Within a week Parícutin had a cone 550 feet high. Two years later it had reached 1500 feet.

Turbulent waters

▲ Tsunami are tidal waves caused by offshore earthquakes or volcanic eruptions. When Krakatoa exploded in 1883 a wall of water 100 feet high swept across Java and Sumatra drowning 36,000 people.

◀ Ground water coming into contact with heated rocks turns into steam. Eventually pressure forces this to the surface as a geyser. 'Old Faithful' in Yellowstone National Park, U.S.A. throws a fountain of boiling water 120 feet into the air once an hour.

Earth's Building Blocks

The crust of the earth is entirely composed of various kinds of rock. Rocks are made of many different minerals. Sometimes the minerals occur as crystals of beautiful shape and colour. But in most rocks individual minerals are difficult to see. Rock formation is a continuous process. The land is constantly being worn away by erosion, whether by wind, ice, rivers or the sea. So in time all rocks are destroyed to be carried away, deposited and eventually formed into new rocks.

We use rocks in a number of different ways. Some are used as building stones. Slate is used for roofing. Coal and oil (a liquid rock) provide fuel. Where certain minerals such as iron ore are found in large quantities they are mined for industry. Even the soil, which is such a vital part of the biosphere, is largely made of ground-up rock fragments.

The world's largest cave
The study of caves is called spelaeology. Most caves form in limestone. The world's largest cave is the 'Big Room' of the Carlsbad Caverns in New Mexico. It is 4000 ft long, 600 ft wide and 300 ft high and has a staggering array of stalagmites and stalactites.

How rocks are formed
There are three main groups of rocks: *Igneous* rocks form when magma cools and becomes solid. Igneous comes from a Greek word meaning 'fire-like'. Within the crust the magma cools slowly and crystals have time to develop, as in granite. When the magma escapes at the surface as lava-flows it cools more quickly to form rocks such as basalt.

▶ The basalt of Fingals' Cave probably flowed into a lake. As it cooled it fractured into these regular columns.

Sedimentary rocks are formed when other rocks are worn away. The fragments are deposited in layers, called strata, by wind, ice, rivers and the sea. In time pressure fuses the sediments together. Sandstone, chalk and limestone are sedimentary rocks.

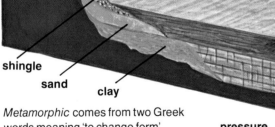

shingle

sand

clay

limestone

Metamorphic comes from two Greek words meaning 'to change form'. These rocks develop under great heat or pressure. Both sedimentary and igneous rocks can change in this way. Limestone will change into marble and clay into slate. Even a hard rock like granite can melt and its crystals rearrange into layers in a rock called gneiss.

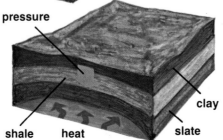

pressure

shale   **heat**

clay

slate

Limestone is formed from the solidified calcium carbonate shells of sea creatures. The solid calcium carbonate dissolves in slightly acidic rain-water. Lines of weakness in the rock are attacked by the water and enlarged to create an underground system of channels. Surface rivers disappear down the vertical potholes and follow these channels, eroding them still further. Eventually a weird and spectacular system of caves is formed.

Pot-holing can be very exciting but it is also dangerous. It is cold, damp and dark underground, so warm clothing and powerful lamps are needed. A safety helmet, a whistle and a first-aid kit are also essential.

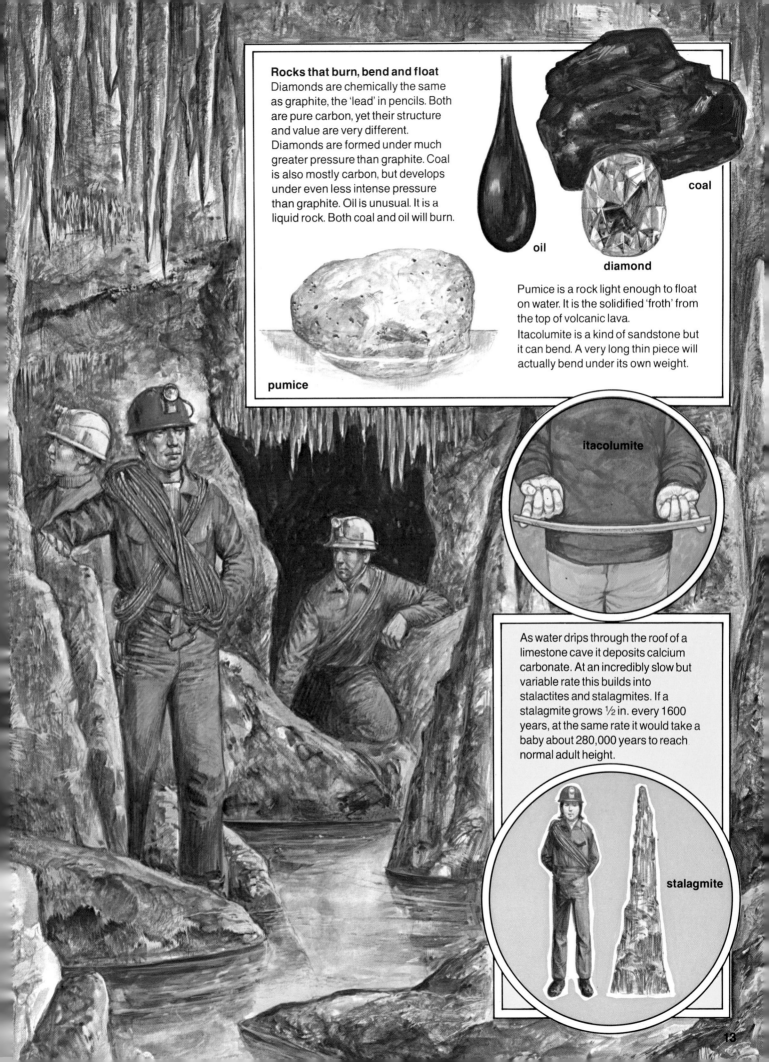

Rocks that burn, bend and float

Diamonds are chemically the same as graphite, the 'lead' in pencils. Both are pure carbon, yet their structure and value are very different. Diamonds are formed under much greater pressure than graphite. Coal is also mostly carbon, but develops under even less intense pressure than graphite. Oil is unusual. It is a liquid rock. Both coal and oil will burn.

oil

coal

diamond

Pumice is a rock light enough to float on water. It is the solidified 'froth' from the top of volcanic lava.

Itacolumite is a kind of sandstone but it can bend. A very long thin piece will actually bend under its own weight.

pumice

itacolumite

As water drips through the roof of a limestone cave it deposits calcium carbonate. At an incredibly slow but variable rate this builds into stalactites and stalagmites. If a stalagmite grows ½ in. every 1600 years, at the same rate it would take a baby about 280,000 years to reach normal adult height.

stalagmite

Crumpling the earth's crust

Fold mountains develop from compression in the earth's crust. Try pushing a piece of paper with both hands moving towards each other. The paper will crumple up into a series of folds. Fold mountains are formed in just the same way. Layers of sediment deposited under water are scooped out and buckled into mountain ranges as the crustal plates move together. After folding, the sediments take up less room than when they were horizontal so the compression is relieved.

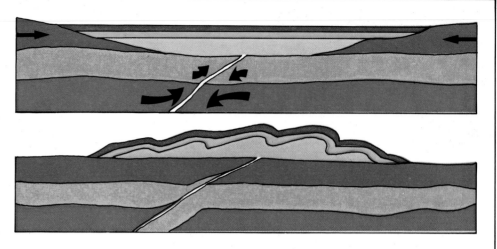

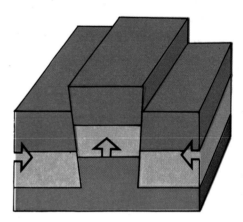

Fracturing the crust

When the compression in the crust is so great that the rocks cannot fold any more, then great fractures or faults develop. Faulting is also caused by tension when the crust is pulled apart. Along the line of the fault, blocks of land are pushed up vertically, so the mountains that result are called block mountains. Table Mountain in South Africa is a block mountain and has the characteristic flat top and steep sides.

Large lungs and short legs

At high altitudes, air pressure is lower so there is less oxygen available for breathing. People living under these conditions tend to be short and stocky in build. Their blood contains extra red cells so they can make maximum use of the oxygen available. For this reason Kip Keino, who came from the highlands of Kenya, had little difficulty winning the gold medal in the 1500 metres at the Mexico City Olympic Games.

The roof of the world

The Himalayas are the highest mountains in the world. They were formed 35 million years ago when India moved north towards mainland Asia. Many mountaineers visiting the Himalayas suffer the effects of mountain sickness — headaches, nausea and giddiness — until they become acclimatized. The Sherpas who live in the high valleys of Nepal are used as porters on mountaineering expeditions. However, even they have to use oxygen equipment on the highest peaks.

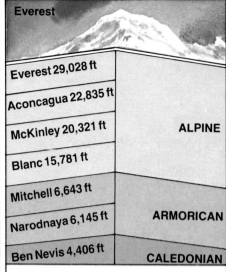

Ups and Downs

The greatest difference in height of the earth's crust is over 65,000 ft. This is from the top of Mount Everest (29,028 ft) to the bottom of the Challenger Deep in the Pacific (36,198 ft). Although man has climbed to the top of Everest the deepest he has so far ventured under the sea is 35,814 ft. This was in a bathyscaphe, a specially built diving vessel. The lowest point on the land's surface is the shoreline on the Dead Sea. This is 1287 ft below sea level.

Apart from volcanoes, mountains are formed either by folding or faulting of the earth's crust. Mountain building is a very long, slow process and not the result of some major catastrophe. The world's oldest mountains have worn away. Today they are the low-lying areas which form the stable centres of the crustal plates. By contrast the youngest mountains are found at the edges of the plates. Clearly the movement of the earth's plates is also involved in mountain building.

Everest

Everest 29,028 ft	
Aconcagua 22,835 ft	
McKinley 20,321 ft	ALPINE
Blanc 15,781 ft	
Mitchell 6,643 ft	
Narodnaya 6,145 ft	ARMORICAN
Ben Nevis 4,406 ft	CALEDONIAN

Building up and wearing down
From the moment mountains start being uplifted, erosion begins to wear them away. The youngest mountains in the world are also the highest and most rugged. The older mountains are, the less high and more rounded they become. Mountains have formed at least three times in the earth's history. Caledonian mountains formed 400 million years ago. Armorican mountains formed 270 million years ago. Alpine mountains formed 35 million years ago.

Working under pressure
Penetrating the depths of the oceans is difficult. Of course divers cannot breathe under water without special breathing apparatus. But, as the divers go deeper, so the water pressure increases. At great depths, divers need protection from the pressure. This 'jim' suit weighs half a ton and costs around $60,000. It can be used as deep as 1500 ft.

15

Rising waters

Floods occur when so much rain falls that rivers burst their banks and overflow, often destroying crops and livestock. The worst ever floods were in China in 1931. About 3,700,000 people were killed and millions more made homeless.

Flooding may be controlled by the building of dams or barrages across rivers. A barrier across the Thames is now being constructed at Silvertown. Many parts of London would be endangered if a major flood occurred before its completion.

Wet and Windy

Whatever the weather may bring – rain, snow, wind or blistering heat – it all forms within the troposphere. This is the lowest lay of the atmosphere, extending up to about 7 miles above the earth's surface. However there would be no weather at all without the sun. This heats the earth's surface, but the heating is not the same over the whole of the planet. These differences in air temperature cause differences in air pressure. Where warm air rises it creates low pressure. Where cold air sinks back to earth, it creates high pressure. Air moves from areas of high pressure to areas of low pressure, creating winds. (Wind is simply moving air.) Warm air can hold more moisture than cold air. As the warm air rises, it cools and the moisture it contains condenses and falls as rain.

Killer winds

Tropical storms are giant spirals of very strong winds which develop around an area of intense low pressure. They are accompanied by torrential rain, thunder and lightning. At their height they are extremely destructive. But at the centre in the 'eye' there is almost no wind. Hurricanes and typhoons develop over the sea and usually drive a great hurricane wave ahead of their path. These storms may be 350 miles across and have wind speeds of 125 mph. Tornadoes are smaller but far more violent, beginning and ending very quickly. The funnel of whirling air, reaching speeds of 500 mph, leaves a path of disaster only 1200 ft wide.

Tacoma Narrows bridge
In 1940, high winds hit the Tacoma Narrows bridge, U.S.A. The bridge tried to take off like an aircraft and, as a result, shook itself to pieces.

A drop in the ocean

Moisture evaporates from the oceans. It is held in the air as invisible water vapour. This cools and condenses into droplets which can be seen as clouds. The water droplets get bigger until their weight causes them to fall as rain. Eventually rainwater makes its way back to the oceans. Sometimes, as in thunder clouds, violent uprushes of air carry the droplets upwards until they freeze into pellets of ice. These fall as hail. One hailstone measuring 7 ins across fell in Kansas, U.S.A. in 1970.

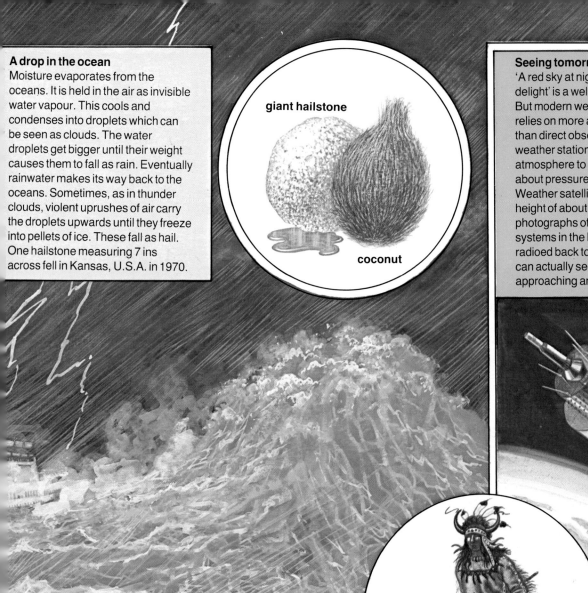

giant hailstone

coconut

Seeing tomorrow's weather today

'A red sky at night is a shepherd's delight' is a well-know proverb. But modern weather forecasting relies on more advanced techniques than direct observation. Automatic weather stations are sent into the atmosphere to collect information about pressure and temperature. Weather satellites orbit the earth at a height of about 450 miles. From them photographs of clouds and weather systems in the lower atmosphere are radioed back to earth. Weather men can actually see the type of weather approaching any particular area.

isobars

warm front

cold front

occluded front

'Here is the weather forecast'

A weather map shows all the information supplied by a number of weather stations, at the same moment. Each station is shown by a circle. By studying a series of these weather maps it is possible to forecast the weather for a short time ahead.

⌇ **thunderstorm**

, **drizzle**

• **rain**

▽ **shower**

✳ **snow**

△ **hail**

≡ **fog**

temperature — wind direction

weather conditions — cloud cover — wind speed

Man-made weather

For centuries people have attempted to influence the weather. The Indian rain dancer tries to persuade his gods to send rain. Cloud seeding is a modern method for making rain. A cloud has to be found which could produce rain if conditions were right. An aircraft drops chemicals into the cloud. Some rain has been made this way but the method is unreliable and very costly.

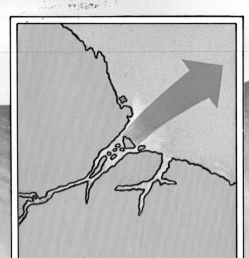

The mighty Amazon
The Amazon is the world's greatest river. It is 4,050 miles long. It drains the largest river basin and has the longest tributary, the Madeira river. It also has the greatest outflow of any river, averaging 4 million cubic feet per second and carrying fresh water far out into the Atlantic.

Raging waters
The world's highest waterfall is Angel Falls on the river Carrao in Venezuela. The water drops a spectacular 3,212 feet.
   Waterfalls are caused by obstructions in the river bed. Many occur where a band of hard rock is followed by softer rock which is more easily worn away. Waterfalls are only a temporary feature as eventually they wear away the obstruction completely.

Rivers, Lakes and Marshes

Rivers erode the land in many ways. Water can dissolve certain minerals in the rocks. Where water is forced into cracks and crevices, it prises off pieces of rock. Rock fragments then scratch and scrape away more of the river bed. All the time the material being carried by the river, its load, is itself being broken down into smaller pieces. This is later deposited downstream. The Mississippi carries about 500 million tons of material into the Gulf of Mexico each year, and the river's delta is growing rapidly. Although rivers can be useful to us, we may create problems if we interfere with their natural flow. Every year the Nile floods brought life-giving water and a layer of fertile mud to the lower valley. Now the Aswan dam holds back the flood water to provide year-round irrigation. But without the river's deposit of mud, the soil is not so fertile and the farmers must buy expensive fertilizers instead.

The lower section of a river is the plain stage. Here the river meanders over a wide, flat flood plain. Sometimes a river will cut a straight channel across the neck of a meander to leave a backwater known as an oxbow lake. There is little erosion in this part of the river. It needs all its energy to carry its load, some of which is dropped on the river bed. When a river floods, part of its load is deposited over the flood plain as fertile mud or alluvium.

River marshes develop wherever the land is low-lying, flat and wet. The greatest marshes in the world are the Pripet Marshes in the U.S.S.R. They cover an area of 29,000 miles.

The remainder of a river's load is deposited when it enters the sea. Here it builds up into either estuary banks or a delta. A delta develops where more material is deposited than is removed by the action of the sea. Deltas gradually build up so that the land spreads out into the sea. Some deltas are fan-shaped like the Nile's. The Greeks called the Nile's mouth delta because it resembled their Greek letter delta, written Δ. The name has stuck for all deltas, whatever their shape!

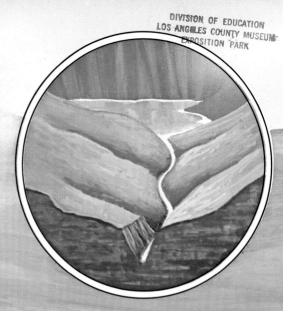

The upper section of a river is the torrent stage, in which the young river rushes down a steep slope, splashing and bubbling over boulders in its bed. All the power of the river is concentrated on eroding its valley downwards. So the valley is narrow and steep-sided and is shaped like a V. The young river is easily deflected by obstacles in its way, so it follows a winding course. Rapids and waterfalls often used for hydro-electric power are found here.

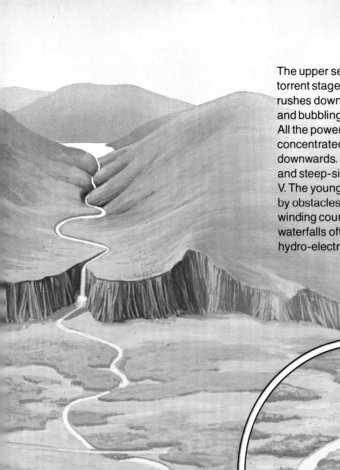

The middle section of a river is the valley stage. The river is still eroding its valley but as the slope is less steep, the water cuts sideways into its banks, rather than downwards. At the valley stage, bends become larger because the current is strongest on the outside of the bend. The bends are called meanders. They wear away the ends of the spurs, the tongues of higher ground between the meanders. So the valley floor becomes much wider.

A valuable servant
▲ Water transport is the cheapest way of moving heavy, bulky goods. The Rhine is the busiest river in the world. Every year motorized barges carry 200 million tons of cargo.
◀ Rivers are very useful as route-ways. Lewis and Clark, the first explorers to cross North America, followed river valleys to make their way through the Rocky Mountains.
▶ Rivers provide irrigation and power. The Grand Coulee dam in the U.S.A. holds back some of the Columbia River to form Lake Roosevelt. The water irrigates farming land and hydro-electric power is generated at the dam.

Crisis! World's major cities flooded!

The polar regions are the coldest places on the earth. Both are covered by vast ice caps. It is estimated that there is 21 million cubic miles of ice covering Antarctica alone. This represents considerably more fresh water than there is in the rest of the world. If the ice caps melted a tremendous amount of water would be released into the sea. This would raise the level of the oceans by 230 feet – enough to flood all the world's major ports and cities.

Building on ice

▲ On the ice caps, buildings erected for research stations or defence bases soon become buried by snow and drift. Only chimneys, air vents and radio masts show above the surface.

South of the Arctic lies the permafrost, a zone of permanent frozen ground. During the brief summer the surface layer thaws out becoming a shifting waterlogged mass. It can buckle roads and railway lines. To prevent this happening to the Alaskan oil pipeline, sections of it were laid above ground on supports. The ground under the pumping stations had to be refrigerated to stop the soil from melting.

Drinking icebergs?

Towering vertical ice cliffs look very spectacular. Sometimes huge blocks break off and float away as icebergs. These become a menace when they drift into shipping lanes.

About 99% of the world's fresh water is locked away in the ice caps. It might be possible to tow icebergs from Antarctica to places like California, Australia, and the Middle East where water is in short supply. Large tugs would tow the icebergs which would probably be wrapped in polythene to preserve the water. Although the cost would be enormous it would be cheaper than that of making fresh water by desalinating sea water.

Icebound!

In the past ice covered a much greater area than it does now. The barren, lake-studded wastes of North America, Northern Europe and the U.S.S.R. could only have been made by an enormous ice sheet. The ice spread during a time we call the Ice Age, which probably started about a million years ago. Since then the ice has advanced and retreated four times. Some people believe we are now in a period between ice ages and that the ice will advance again in the future. However, ice caps are unusual in the earth's history and the earth may now be returning to its more normal warmer conditions. If so, there will be a complete melting of the ice caps.

Nobody knows why ice ages occur. It has been suggested they are due to 'sun spots', which cause the amount of radiation (heat) from the sun to decrease. This would lead to a change in the earth's climate.

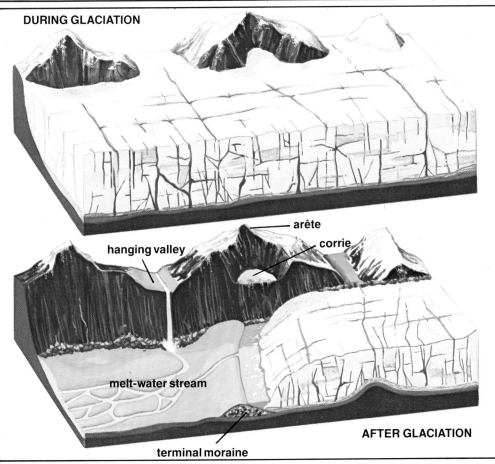

DURING GLACIATION

arête

hanging valley

corrie

melt-water stream

AFTER GLACIATION

terminal moraine

Rivers of ice

Valley glaciers are rivers of ice found in mountain areas. They are fed from permanent snow fields high in the mountains. The surface of a glacier is not smooth but buckled by pressure ridges and broken by great cracks called crevasses. These occur because unlike water, ice cannot adjust to the shape of the land without breaking. As a glacier moves it becomes embedded with rock fragments which act as a giant file, scraping and eroding the land. Being solid a glacier carves for itself a broad, steep-sided, U-shaped valley. Any obstacles in its path, such as spurs, are worn away so straight valleys are cut.

When a glacier melts, its load is deposited as moraine. A terminal moraine is a long ridge that builds up at the snout (end) of a glacier. Melt-water streams drain away the water. These may develop into great rivers. The source of the river Rhône in France is a glacier.

The Empty Lands

About one eighth of the world's land surface is covered by deserts. The Sahara in North Africa is the largest desert at 3,200,000 square miles. In it there are three types of desert surface, solid rock, stony and sandy. Rocks in deserts are broken down by rapid heating and cooling. Temperatures soar during the day but fall rapidly at night as there is no cloud cover to keep in the heat. Wind shifts the rock fragments and sand. Armed with grains of sand the wind becomes a powerful erosive force, etching rocks into strange shapes.

Some people think that the desert regions were extended by bad farming methods in the past. We know the Romans used to cultivate parts of the northern Sahara where today nothing will grow.

Swirling sands
When the wind blows unchecked across the desert it picks up the dry grains of sand and dust and creates suffocating sand-storms. These may completely alter the surface of the desert, causing travellers to lose their way. The winds can carry the sand great distances. Dunes have even built up in the Canary Islands from sand blown over 200 miles from the Sahara Desert.

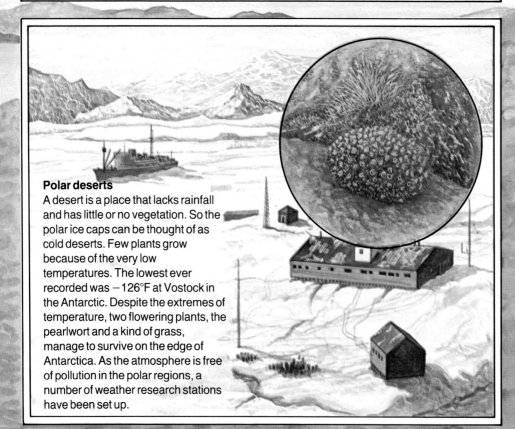

Polar deserts
A desert is a place that lacks rainfall and has little or no vegetation. So the polar ice caps can be thought of as cold deserts. Few plants grow because of the very low temperatures. The lowest ever recorded was −126°F at Vostock in the Antarctic. Despite the extremes of temperature, two flowering plants, the pearlwort and a kind of grass, manage to survive on the edge of Antarctica. As the atmosphere is free of pollution in the polar regions, a number of weather research stations have been set up.

Movement across sandy deserts is very difficult. Camels with their superb adaptations to desert conditions are the traditional means of transport. They store fat in their humps and water in a second stomach. Large, padded feet prevent them sinking into the sand. Long eyelashes protect their eyes during sand-storms. Landrovers are the modern equivalent of camels. But unlike camels they can get stuck in the sand or break down!
Sandy deserts are not so common as many people believe. As the sand is dry and loose the wind is constantly changing the desert's surface. Where the wind blows mainly from one direction dunes build up. The sand can even blow across an oasis and destroy it.

A rose that isn't a flower
This rare and beautiful 'desert rose' is in fact a cluster of barytes crystals. These roses can sometimes be found in the desert sands of Oklahoma, U.S.A. Barytes, also called 'heavy spar' because of its weight, is a mineral used in making white paint and paper.

Monuments to the past
Monument Valley in Arizona, U.S.A. is famous for its stark, flat-topped hills and vertical pillars of rock. These are called mesas and buttes. Their flat tops show the original height of the land surface. Wind and water have cut into this, eroding the land to its present level. The mesas and buttes remain because they stand up better to erosion.

Brief lives
Only plants able to withstand drought conditions can survive in deserts. Cacti store water in their thick, fleshy stems. Many plants have very short life cycles. When the brief rains come the seeds germinate, the plant flowers, scatters its seeds and dies. Many desert animals survive the heat by hiding in burrows during the day. The burrowing frog of central Australia only appears above ground during a rare rainstorm. In a matter of days the frog feeds, mates and lays its eggs. The hatching tadpoles develop very quickly. Then the frog absorbs water until it becomes bloated. It burrows into the sand and secretes a membrane around itself to prevent water loss.

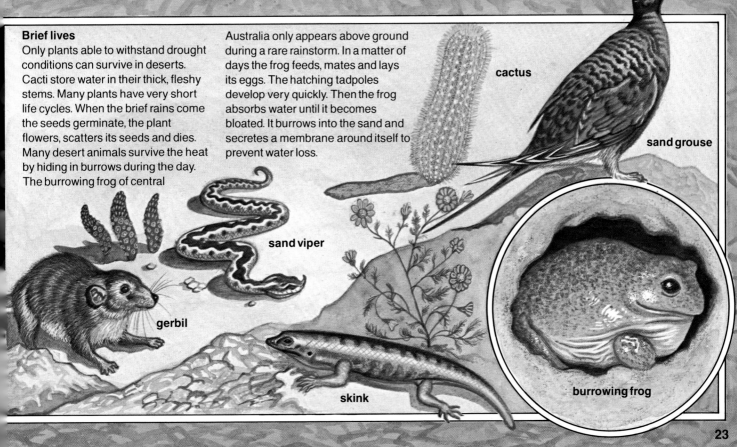

cactus

sand grouse

sand viper

gerbil

skink

burrowing frog

23

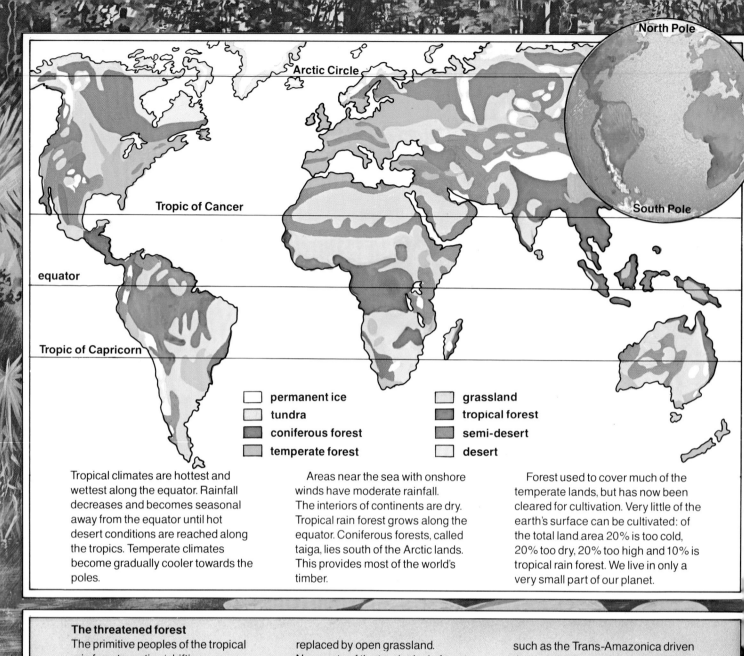

North Pole

Arctic Circle

Tropic of Cancer

South Pole

equator

Tropic of Capricorn

☐ permanent ice	☐ grassland	
☐ tundra	☐ tropical forest	
☐ coniferous forest	☐ semi-desert	
☐ temperate forest	☐ desert	

Tropical climates are hottest and wettest along the equator. Rainfall decreases and becomes seasonal away from the equator until hot desert conditions are reached along the tropics. Temperate climates become gradually cooler towards the poles.

Areas near the sea with onshore winds have moderate rainfall. The interiors of continents are dry. Tropical rain forest grows along the equator. Coniferous forests, called taiga, lies south of the Arctic lands. This provides most of the world's timber.

Forest used to cover much of the temperate lands, but has now been cleared for cultivation. Very little of the earth's surface can be cultivated: of the total land area 20% is too cold, 20% too dry, 20% too high and 10% is tropical rain forest. We live in only a very small part of our planet.

The threatened forest

The primitive peoples of the tropical rain forest practise 'shifting cultivation'. Small patches are cleared of trees and cultivated until the soil is exhausted. The forest invades again but grows less thickly. If this keeps happening, in time the forest may be replaced by open grassland. Now parts of the tropical rain forests are being 'developed'. Today exploration for minerals and greater demand for tropical timber are bringing more people to the forests. New cities are being built and roads such as the Trans-Amazonica driven through the forest. Although these may bring short-term prosperity to the regions, in the long-term they could be disastrous both for the future of the forests and for the rest of the world.

The Teeming Forests

The great forests of the world are vital in maintaining the delicate balance that exists between all living things. Like all green plants trees absorb water, take carbon dioxide from the air, and use the sun's energy to convert these into carbohydrates (their food). This process is called photosynthesis. Oxygen, which is essential to animal life, is produced as a by-product. So the forests can be thought of as great oxygen factories. Felling of trees on a large scale could reduce the amount of oxygen in the air.

In most forests much moisture is lost through the leaves. This is carried into the atmosphere, eventually falling as rain. If forests are cut down, then less rain will fall and the vegetation will become poorer. Heat is also released through leaves. In a year the leaves in 10 square feet of tropical forest release enough energy to keep a one-kilowatt fire burning for 9½ hours!

Coco de Mer

coconut

General Sherman

Record-breakers
'General Sherman' is the largest tree in the world. It is 300 ft tall and measures 100 ft around its trunk. The tree is a sequoia, a type of conifer, found in California.
The Coco de Mer, a type of coconut, is the world's largest seed. It can weigh up to 40 lbs.

Tropical rain forest grows where there is over 80 ins of rain a year and constant high temperatures of about 82°F. The forest is dense, evergreen and has a great variety of broadleaved plants. The trees often grow tall and straight. Their tops form a canopy through which only thin shafts of light penetrate to the forest floor. Here there is little undergrowth. Elsewhere the forest has a layered appearance, with tangled undergrowth and small trees of varying heights. Above them all stand the forest giants, 200 ft tall and with great buttresses for support. Lianas and creepers festoon the trees and the whole forest teems with wildlife.

25

Inner Space

Water covers two-thirds of our planet's surface. Yet it is only in the last hundred years that we have really begun to study the ocean depths and to take advantage of the riches the seas have to offer. There are valuable mineral resources including oil, manganese, copper and cobalt. Some occur as nodules the size of tennis balls. These are sucked to the surface by mining vessels like giant vacuum cleaners. Plankton are microscopic animals living in the oceans. They are rich in protein. Perhaps they could be farmed and become an important food.

The waters of the oceans are never still. Tides are caused by the moon and, to a lesser extent, the sun pulling on the earth's gravity. This results in two bulges in the oceans on opposite sides of the earth. Each high tide is 12 hours 25 minutes after the one before.

Salty seas

People cannot drink sea water because of its high salt content. Too much sends us insane. But some sea birds such as the gannet have developed a gland in their nose which extracts the salt and empties it back into the sea. The salt in sea water is mainly sodium chloride with smaller amounts of magnesium, calcium and potassium.

The relentless waves

Waves are caused by the wind. They attack cliff faces, hurling boulders and pebbles against them. The foot of the cliff is at last worn away and the overhanging rock collapses. So the cliff recedes.

Bays are formed where the rocks are easily worn away. Resistant rocks stand out as headlands. Caves develop along any line of weakness such as a joint. Sometimes caves cut right through a headland to form an arch. If the roof falls a stack is left jutting out of the sea.

Sand and shingle are carried along the coast by waves. Groynes are sometimes built across holiday beaches to prevent all the sand from being swept away. Sometimes, where there is a promontory or an inlet, the waves may build the sand and shingle into a spit or bar. These are underwater sandbanks visible at low tide.

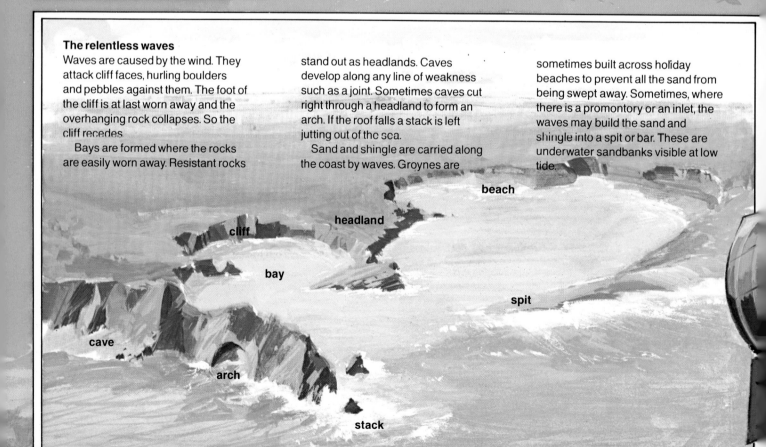

beach

headland

cliff

bay

spit

cave

arch

stack

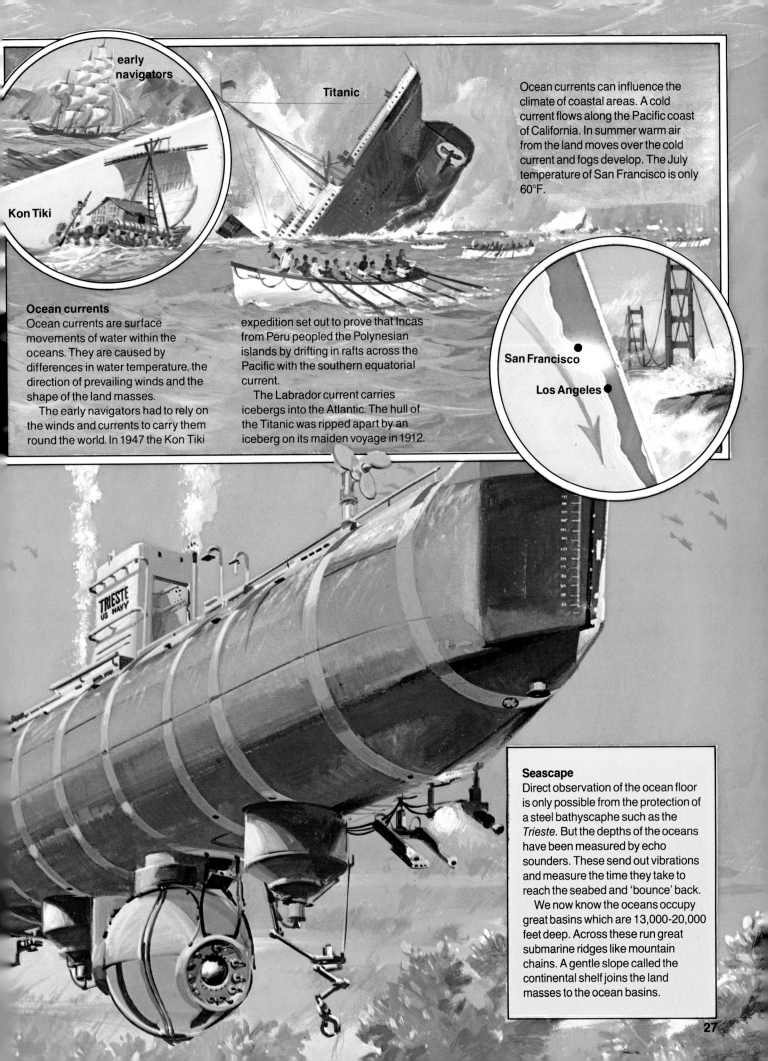

early navigators

Kon Tiki

Titanic

Ocean currents can influence the climate of coastal areas. A cold current flows along the Pacific coast of California. In summer warm air from the land moves over the cold current and fogs develop. The July temperature of San Francisco is only 60°F.

San Francisco

Los Angeles

Ocean currents

Ocean currents are surface movements of water within the oceans. They are caused by differences in water temperature, the direction of prevailing winds and the shape of the land masses.

The early navigators had to rely on the winds and currents to carry them round the world. In 1947 the Kon Tiki expedition set out to prove that Incas from Peru peopled the Polynesian islands by drifting in rafts across the Pacific with the southern equatorial current.

The Labrador current carries icebergs into the Atlantic. The hull of the Titanic was ripped apart by an iceberg on its maiden voyage in 1912.

TRIESTE
US NAVY

Seascape

Direct observation of the ocean floor is only possible from the protection of a steel bathyscaphe such as the *Trieste.* But the depths of the oceans have been measured by echo sounders. These send out vibrations and measure the time they take to reach the seabed and 'bounce' back.

We now know the oceans occupy great basins which are 13,000-20,000 feet deep. Across these run great submarine ridges like mountain chains. A gentle slope called the continental shelf joins the land masses to the ocean basins.

Wave power

The movement of ocean waves could be harnessed for power in the future. Experiments have already been carried out using large rafts of floating vanes which rock up and down with the waves. Their movement drives generators to produce electricity. This can be brought ashore by cable. The rafts need to be sited where there are always large waves, possibly in the Atlantic.

Time is running out

Coal, oil and natural gas are fossil fuels. They stored the sun's energy millions of years ago. By burning them we release that energy. Coal

formed from the decaying plant life of huge forests, oil from minute sea creatures. These fossil fuels are today the world's chief sources of energy. Although there are sufficient reserves for some time to come, we are using them at a rate over 100,000 times the speed at which they are now being formed. So there is no hope of replacing them. Burning these fuels releases more and more carbon dioxide into the air. This helps trap the heat from the sun and is slowly increasing the earth's temperature. It is estimated by the time we have used all the reserves of these fuels, the temperature will have increased sufficiently to melt the world's ice caps.

Switching on the sun

The sun is the greatest source of energy available to man. But solar energy techniques for large-scale use are still in an experimental stage. Solar panels have been built into houses to reduce domestic fuel bills. They are most successful in countries where there are long hours of sunshine. The world's first solar furnace is in the Pyrenees. Here screens carrying 11,000 mirrors reflect the sun's heat onto a huge curved mirror below. This focuses the heat onto a furnace. In future, satellite power stations may harness the sun's energy and beam it to earth.

The Energy Storehouse

For millions of years the sun's energy has supported life on earth. In the unimaginably distant future the sun may engulf the earth and destroy it. But long before that we may well have destroyed our own planet. The human race has inhabited earth for less than a million years. Yet in that time by our ignorance and greed we have interfered with and upset the delicate balance of nature. Soils have been destroyed, deserts created, rivers poisoned, the atmosphere polluted and the earth's resources exploited at an alarming rate. In particular energy resources are fast running out: we have relied too much on fossil fuels. Yet there is energy all around us – in the wind and running water, the waves and tides and ultimately the sun itself. These forms of energy will not run out, nor will they cause pollution. We need to develop the techniques to use these alternative sources before it is too late.

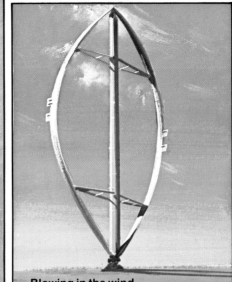

Blowing in the wind
Wind and water both have kinetic energy, the energy of movement. Wind power is cheap but unreliable. Traditionally windmills are connected directly to machinery which stops when the wind dies down. But the wind could drive a generator which would feed electricity into huge storage batteries.

Nuclear energy – mixed blessing?
Nuclear energy is used to make electricity. Although the raw materials, such as uranium, are costly only small quantities are needed to produce enormous amounts of energy. But many people are concerned about the dangers of nuclear power. Large amounts of deadly radioactive waste are produced. How do we dispose of these with complete safety? Despite strict safety measures, accidents can and do happen at nuclear power stations.

Small nuclear reactors are also used to power ships and submarines.

Some useful words

Air pressure Although air is invisible, it has weight. At sea level, the amount of air pressing down on you is almost the same as having 6 medium-sized people balanced on your head. Air pressure increases with depth, e.g. under the oceans. It decreases with height, e.g. up mountains.

Alluvium Fine-grained rock fragments carried by rivers and dropped either over their flood plains or at sea.

Bar A ridge of sand and shingle formed across a bay or the mouth of a river. The sediment is deposited when the current carrying it is slowed down in some way.

Desalination The process of removing salt from sea water to make it into fresh water.

Erosion The constant gradual wearing away of the land by various natural forces such as water, ice and wind.

Fault A fracture in the earth's crust. The two sides of the fracture usually move slightly so that the rocks on either side do not match exactly.

Lianas Climbing plants found in tropical rain forests. The stems of lianas are thick and woody and they twist around the trunks and branches of trees.

Magma The molten rock which is found below the solid rock of the earth's crust.

Plate tectonics The theory that explains why earthquakes, volcanoes and mountains occur. If you think of the earth's crust like the hard shell of a nut which has been cracked in many places, the broken pieces are the plates. The plate edges are constantly in motion, jostling against each other, so earth movements happen around the edges of the plates.

Photosynthesis The process by which all green plants take in water, extract carbon dioxide from the air and, with energy from the sun, turn these into carbohydrates, their food. Oxygen is produced as a waste product.

Relief The difference in height of any part of the earth's surface.

River basin The total area drained by a river and all its tributaries.

Spit This is similar to a bar except that one end is attached to the land.

Stalactites and stalagmites Columns of deposited mineral matter. Stalactites hang downwards. Stalagmites grow upwards.

Tributary A smaller river draining into a larger river.

Things to do

Collecting fossils and minerals

The only equipment you need is a hammer and chisel to chip away pieces of rock, and a strong bag to carry these and any specimens you find. A geology map and a notebook and pencil to record where specimens were found are useful. You will also need a good reference book, preferably in colour, so that you can identify what you find. Cliffs and river banks expose the rock so these are the best places to look for specimens. You can also find signs of folding and faulting in such places. Quarries, road and railway cuttings are also good places, but you need to be very careful and always ask permission first of all.

Many local museums have rock and fossil collections and the curator will be glad to help if you have any problems identifying a specimen. If you are ever in London the Geological Museum and the Natural History Museum are two excellent places to visit.

Studying a stream

Follow it upstream to find its source. What is it like? Try to measure the width of the stream and the width of its valley floor. What is the difference? If the stream is shallow you could wade in to measure its depth. Is the depth the same over the complete width of the stream? To find out how fast a stream is flowing, measure and mark 2 points 5 metres apart on the bank. Throw a stick into the middle of the stream and time how long it takes to travel between the marked points. Can you see how the stream is actually eroding its valley and whether it is undercutting the bank?

Books to read

The Guinness Book of Records contains many facts and figures about the earth. There are some quite inexpensive pocket guides on geology, weather, the seashore and fossils all published by Warne and Co. in the Observer series. Other books include:

Wooley. *Spotter's Guide to Rocks and Minerals.* Usborne Pocket Books.
Kircaldy. *Fossils.* Blandford Colour Series.
Kircaldy. *Rocks and Minerals.* Blandford Colour Series.
Hammersley. *Approaches to Environmental Studies, The World of Water.* Blandford.
Davis. *Inside the Earth.* Macdonald Visual Books.
Parsons. *Oceans and Deserts.* Macdonald New Reference Library.
Dalton. *The Weather.* Priory Press Limited.

Forecasting the weather

Clouds show that there is moisture in the atmosphere, so they are a fairly accurate means of forecasting the weather. Cirrus clouds look like thin feathery streaks, and are sometimes called 'mare's tails'. They form above 20,000 ft and are made of ice crystals. The air temperature at this height is below freezing. They are often the sign of approaching bad weather. Stratus cloud occurs much lower, generally below 6,500 ft. It looks like a uniform grey sheet and may bring light rain or drizzle. If it becomes thicker and much darker it is called nimbostratus and will give heavy rain or snow, depending on the temperature. Cumulus clouds are billowy in appearance. They have a low, level base but can tower to great heights. Shallow fair weather cumulus may develop on warm, sunny days. Towering cumulus clouds bring showers of rain. The huge, very dark cumulonimbus clouds, sometimes with anvil-shaped heads, produce very heavy rain, hail and thunder storms.

cumulus

Finding out about the Earth

It is not difficult to find out more about the planet on which you live because the information is all around you. Look carefully at the area in which you live. Is it hilly or flat? Look at a geology map and try to relate the rocks to the landscape. Has a river helped to shape the land? Can you find out what conditions may have been like in the past? Compare your home area with somwhere you visit on holiday.

Try to visit some limestone country and join an organized tour through a cave system to feel what it is like to go down into the earth. But do not try to go pot-holing by yourself – it is very dangerous!

Make a simple barometer

Slightly warm a bottle. Stretch a piece of balloon rubber tightly across the top and fix it securely in place with glue and a rubber band. Glue a small piece of balsa wood to the centre of the rubber. Then glue a drinking straw to the balsa wood. This acts as a pointer. Fix a scale to a wall behind the pointer and you will be able to see changes in air pressure. As the pressure increases the rubber expands and the pointer moves along the scale. Rising pressure usually means fine weather to come.

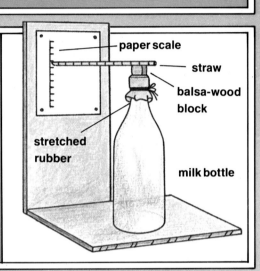

paper scale
straw
balsa-wood block
stretched rubber
milk bottle

▲Quartz, also called rock crystal, is a common mineral found in many rocks.

◀Calcite is another common mineral found particularly in sedimentary rock.

▶Galena is lead ore. It is very heavy.

◀ Haematite (kidney ore) is a very rich form of iron ore.

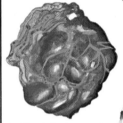

▶Blue john is a variety of fluorspar. It is used to make ornaments and jewellery.

◀Granite often contains traces of several minerals.

Minerals are rarely found in their beautiful crystallized forms shown here. They are usually found as shapeless grains in rock. This granite contains traces of felspar (white), quartz (glassy grains), and mica (black and silver grains).

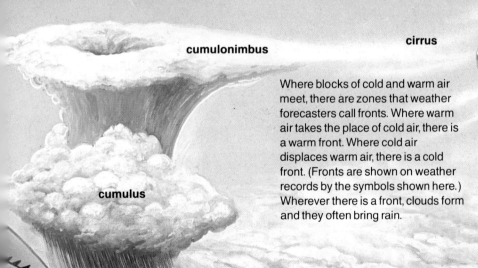

cumulonimbus

cirrus

cumulus

Where blocks of cold and warm air meet, there are zones that weather forecasters call fronts. Where warm air takes the place of cold air, there is a warm front. Where cold air displaces warm air, there is a cold front. (Fronts are shown on weather records by the symbols shown here.) Wherever there is a front, clouds form and they often bring rain.

nimbostratus

stratus

.D FRONT

WARM FRONT

Index

Aconcagua, Mt 15
Alaska 9, 20
Alpine mountains 15
Aluminium 8
Amazon, river 18
Amino acids 7
Angel Falls, Venezuela 18
Arête 21
Armorican mountains 15
Aswan dam 18
Atmosphere 6

Bacteria 7
Barytes 23
Basalt 12
Bathyscaphe 15, 27
Ben Nevis 15
Biosphere 6
Blanc, Mont 15
Block mountains 14
Buttes 23

Cacti 23
Calcite 31
Calcium carbonate 12, 13
Caledonian mountains 15
Camels 22
Carlsbad Caverns, New Mexico 12
Carbon 13
Carbon monoxide 6
Caves 12-13, 26
Chalk 12
Challenger Deep 15
China 16
Clouds 17, 30-1
Coal 8, 12, 13, 28
Continental shelf 27
Corries 21
Crust, earth's 8-9, 12-13, 14
Coco de Mer 25
Currents 27

Deltas 19
Deserts 22-3
Diamond 13
Diving, deep-sea 15, 27

Earthquakes 8-9
Echo-sounding 27
Energy 28-9
Equator 4, 5, 24
Equinoxes 5
Erosion 12, 15, 18-19, 26
Everest, Mt 6, 15

Faulting 14
Fingal's Cave 12
Floods 16, 18, 20
Forests 24-5
Fossils 6, 30
Fossil fuels 28

Frog, burrowing 23

Galaxies 4
Gannet 26
Gas, natural 28
General Sherman (tree) 24
Gerbil 23
Geysers 11
Glaciers 21
Gneiss 12
Grand Coulee Dam 19
Granite 12
Graphite 13

Haematite 31
Hawaii 10
Himalayas 15
Hurricanes 16

Ice 20-1
Icebergs 20, 27
Igneous rock 12
Iron 8, 12
Itacolumite 13

Japan 7
Jupiter 7

Kon Tiki 27
Krakatoa 11

Lava 10-11, 12
Limestone 12, 13
Lipari Islands 10

McKinley, Mt 15
Magma 11, 12
Magnesium 8
Mantle, earth's 8
Marble 12
Mars 7
Mesas 23
Metamorphic rocks 12
Milky Way 4
Minerals 26
Mississippi, river 18
Mitchell, Mt 15
Mohole project 8
Mohorovičić, Andrija 8
Monument Valley, USA 23
Moraine 21
Mountains, formation of 14-15

Narodnaya, Mt 15
Nickel 8
Nile, river 18
Nuclear energy 29

Oceans 26-7
Oil 12, 13, 28
Ox bow lake 19
Oxygen 6, 7, 14, 25
Ozone 6

Pacific Ocean 11, 14
Pangaea 8

Parícutin, Mexico 11
Pelée, Mt 11
Permafrost 20
Photosynthesis 6, 25
Plankton 26
Pluto 7
Polar regions 20-1, 22
Pollution 29
Pressure (atmospheric) 16
Pripet marshes, U.S.S.R. 19
Proteins 7
Pumice 13

Radioactive dating 6
Radioactivity 29
Rain 16, 17
Rivers 18-19

Sahara desert 22
San Andreas fault 8
San Francisco 8, 27
Sand 22-3, 26
Sedimentary rocks 12
Seismographs 9
Sequoia 24
Shells 12
Sherpa 15
Shifting cultivation 24
Silicon 8
Skink 23
Slate 12
Solar energy 28-9
Solar system 4-5, 6-7
Space travel 5
Spelaeology 12
Stalagmites and stalactites 12, 13
Stars 4
Sun 4, 28, 29
Surtsey Island 10

Table Mountain 14
Taiga 24
Thames barrage 16
Tidal waves 11
Tides 26
Titanic 27
Tornadoes 16
Trans-Amazonica 24
Trieste (bathyscaphe) 27
Tropics 5, 24
Typhoons 16

Ultraviolet rays 6
Uranium 29

Venus 7
Vesuvius, Mt 11
Viking space probes 7
Volcanoes 6, 10-11

Water 18-19, 20, 26-7
Water supply 20
Waterfalls 18
Waves 26, 28
Weather 16-17
Winds 16-17, 29